the duck and the mēan pig

a mother duck and her nīne little ducks went fōr a walk. a big mēan pig met them on the rōad. shē tōld the mother duck, "I am a mēan pig. I ēat cans and I ēat bēans. I ēat cars and I ēat tōys. I ēat beds and I ēat bugs."

the mother duck said, "I am not a can ōr a bēan ōr a car ōr a tōy. I am a duck. and I bīte pigs that ar_e mēan."

sō the pig ran. then the mother duck and her

nīn_e little ducks went to the pond.

the end

going to the toy shop

a boy and his mother went to a toy shop. they went to get toys. the boy said, "I like toys. I like big toys."

his mother said, "I do not like big toys. so we will get little toys."

the man in the toy shop said, "we have a lot of toys. we have toys for boys. we have toys for girls.

and wē have tōys fōr dogs." ⟶

the bōy said, "I am not a dog. I am a bōy. and I
līke big tōys." ⟶

stop ⟶

going to the toy shop

a boy and his mother went shopping for toys.

the boy liked big toys. but his mother liked little

toys.

the man in the toy shop said, "I have toys

that you will like. they are big and little."

the boy said, "toys can not be big and little."

the man said, "these toys are big and little."

hē got a little tōy duck and hē mādе it big.

this is the end.

the fat fox and his brother

a fat fox and his brother went into a big box.

the fat fox said, "I hāte to sit in a box."

his brother said, "sitting in a box is not a lot of fun. let's hit the box. I love to hit a box."

the fat fox said, "I will hit the box with this hand and this nōse and this tāil." sō hē hit and hit.

then the fat fox said, "it is getting hot in this

box. let's stop hitting."

his brother said, "let's gō to slēēp. slēēping in a

box is fun." sō they went to slēēp.

this is the end.

the other sīde of the lāke

a bug sat on the shōre of a big lāke. the bug said, "I nēēd to get to the other sīde of this big lāke."

but the bug did not līke to get wet. hē said, "I līke to slēēp and I līke to rīde in a car. but I do not līke to get wet."

the bug did not have a car and hē did not have

a bed. sō hē sat and sat on the shōrₑ of the lākₑ.

stop

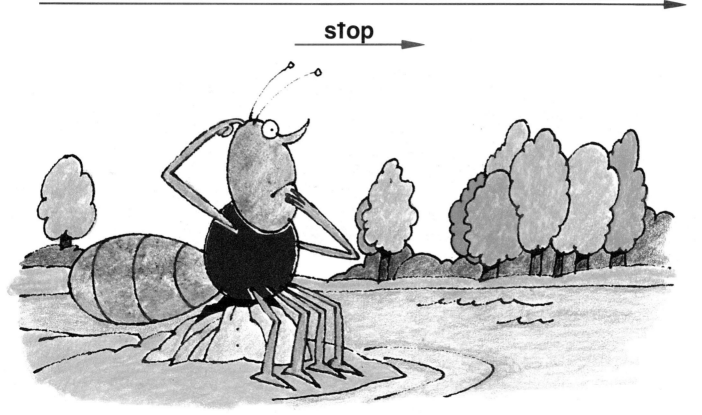

13

the other sīde of the lāke

a bug sat and sat on the shōre of a lāke. hē did

not have a car to tāke him to the other sīde.

then a big ēagle cāme and sat down on the shōre.

the ēagle said, "you are sitting on the shōre and

you are sad."

the bug said, "yes. I am sad. I nēēd to get to

the other sīde of the lāke. I will give you a dīme."

the ēagle said, "yes. givₑ mē a dīmₑ and I will tākₑ you to the other sīdₑ." sō the bug gāvₑ the ēagle a dīmₑ and got on the ēagle. they went ōver the lākₑ.

the end

the pig that bit his leg ➤

a little bug and a pig met on the rōₐd. the pig ➤

said, "I can walk better than you." ➤

the little bug said, "but I can ēat better than ➤

you." then shē bit a log. ➤

the pig said, "I can ēat logs better than you." ➤

the pig went bītₑ, bītₑ, bītₑ and ātₑ the log. ➤

the bug said, "I can bītₑ a pig better than you." ➤

shē bit the pig on the leg. →

the pig said, "I can do better than that." the pig →

gāve his leg a big bīte. →

the bug said, "you bīte pigs better than mē." →

the end →

the cat that talked

a girl had a little cat. shē loved her cat. shē went to the shop with her cat. shē went to the park with her cat. shē loved her cat.

the other dāy, shē was sitting with her cat in the park. shē said, "I love you, little cat. you are never bad. you are fun. but you can not talk to mē and that mākes mē sad."

the cat said, "I can talk to you."

stop

the cat that talked

a girl had a cat. shē loved her cat. shē talked to her cat.

then the cat talked to her. the girl said, "I must bē slēēping. cats can not talk."

the cat said, "you talk to mē. sō I can talk to you."

the girl gāve the cat a big hug. "I never had a

cat that talked." ➤

the cat said, "I never had a cat that talked ➤

either." the girl and the cat talked and talked. ➤

then ann came to the park. she went up to the ➤

girl and said, "can I have that cat?" ➤

the cat said, "I will not go with you." ➤

ann said, "I must be sleeping. cats do not talk. I ➤

will leave this park." and she did. ➤

the end ➤

finding some fun on the moon

some girls went to the moon in a moon ship.

a girl said, "I will find some fun." she walked

and walked. soon she came to a cow.

the moon cow said, "we have lots of fun. come

with me." the girl went with the moon cow to a

pool. the moon cow said, "this is how we have fun

on the moon." she jumped into the pool. and the

girl jumped into the pool.

the girl said, "it is fun to swim on the moon." so the girl and the cow went swimming every day. the girl did not tell the other girls that she went swimming with a moon cow.

the end

will the ōld car start?

a man had an ōld car. the ōld car did not start.

sō the man went down the rōad. soon hē cāme to a

rat.

the man said, "can you start an ōld car?"

the rat said, "nō. rats do not have cars."

sō the man went down the rōad. soon hē cāme to

a big man. hē said, "can you start an ōld car?"

the big man said, "yes. I can but I will not. I
am sitting. I never start cars if I am sitting."

the man said, "you can sit in the car if you can
start it."

sō the big man got in the car and māde the car
start. hē said, "I līke this ōld car. sō I will kēēp
sitting in it." and hē did.

the end

the ōld man fīnds a hōrse

an ōld hōrse was in a barn. hē said, "I am sad.

I can not fīnd a man that will rīde on mē." hē

said to the cat, "have you sēēn a man that will rīde

on mē?"

the cat said, "nō."

an ōld man was walking nēar the barn. hē said to

the cat, "I can not fīnd a hōrse to rīde. have you

sēēn a hōrse that I can rīde?"

the cat said, "yes. hē is in the barn."

then the ōld man walked into the barn. hē went up to the ōld hōrse. the ōld man said, "ōld hōrse, do you līke to gō fōr a rīde?"

the ōld hōrse said, "yes." sō the ōld man and the ōld hōrse went rīding.

the end

rēad the Ītem

1. if the tēacher says "gō," stand up.

bill went fishing

bill lĪked to gō fishing but hē did not get fish. the other bōys went fishing and got lots of fish. a big bōy got fĪve fish. a little bōy got nĪne fish. but bill did not get fish.

bill was mad. hē said, "I wish I had fish lĪke the

other bōys." but nō fish cāme to his līne.

then hē had a tug on his līne. "I have a fish," hē said. but it was not a fish. it was an ōld box.

stop

rēad the Ītem ➔

1. if the tēₐcher says "now," hōld up your hand. ➔

bill went fishiñg ➔

bill went fishiñg with the other bōys. but hē did ➔
not get fĪvₑ fish. hē did not get nĪnₑ fish. hē got ➔
an ōld box. ➔

the other bōys mādₑ fun of bill. "wē havₑ fish ➔
and you do not. you havₑ an ōld box." ➔

bill was sad. hē hit the box. the top fell down. and

bill said, "that box is filled with gōld."

bill was not sad. hē said to the other bōys, "you

havₑ lots of fish, but I havₑ lots of gōld."

this is the end.

rēad the Ītem ➤

1. if the tēacher says "now," hōld up your hands. ➤

an ōld hōrse and an ēagle ➤

an ōld hōrse and an ēagle sat on a hill. the ēagle ➤

said, "it is fun to flȳ. mȳ mother līkes to flȳ. mȳ ➤

brother līkes to flȳ. and I līke to flȳ." ➤

the ōld hōrse said, "can you tēach mē how to ➤

flȳ?" ➤

the ēagle said, "I will flȳ to the top of the

barn." and hē did.

the ōld hōrse said, "I will flȳ to the top of the

barn." sō hē ran down the hill. and hē ran into the

sīde of the barn. hē said, "you did not tēach mē

how to flȳ."

stop

rē_ad the Ītem →

I. when the tē_acher says "do it," pick up your book. →

an ōld hōrs_e and an ē_{agl}e →

an ē_{agl}e was tē_achin͡g an ōld hōrs_e how to flȳ. →

but the ōld hōrs_e did not flȳ. the ōld hōrs_e ran into →

the sīd_e of a barn. →

the ē_{agl}e said, "I will flȳ to the top of the car." →

and hē did. →

but the ōld hōrse did not flȳ to the top of the

car. hē ran into the sīde of the car. hē said, "mȳ

mother and mȳ brother can not flȳ. I can not flȳ."

the ēagle said, "if you can not flȳ, you can not

have fun."

the hōrse said, "I can run with an ēagle on mȳ

back, and that is fun."

sō the ēagle sat on the back of the ōld hōrse and

the ōld hōrse ran. "yes, this is fun," they said.

the end

rēad the Ītems

1. when the tēacher says "gō," pat your ēars.

2. when the tēacher says "do it," touch your fēēt.

the red tooth brush

a girl had a red tooth brush. shē līked her red tooth brush. shē brushed her tēēth six tīmes a dāy. shē said, "mȳ tēēth are whīte. they are sō whīte they shīne līke the moon."

the girl had a dog, but his tēēth did not shīne.

the girl went to brush her tēēth. but shē did not sēē her tooth brush. "I do not sēē mȳ red tooth brush," shē said.

shē went to her mother. "I nēēd mȳ red tooth brush."

but her mother said, "I do not have your red tooth brush."

stop

rēₐd the Ītems ⟶

1. when the tēₐcher says "stand up," pick up your

book.

2. if the tēₐcher says "now," hōld up your hands.

the red tooth brush ⟶

a girl lĪked to brush her tēēth. shē looked fōr

her red tooth brush. but her mother did not haveₑ it.

the girl went back to her room. on the wāy, shē

slipped and fell. shē slipped on her dog. her dog

was brushing his tēēth with her red tooth brush.

the girl said, "you have mȳ red tooth brush."

the dog said, "I līke tēēth that shīne līke the

moon."

the girl smīled and the dog smīled. they said,

"now wē bōth have tēēth that shīne līke the moon."

the end

rēad the Ītems →

1. if the tēacher stands up, touch your hand. →

2. if the tēacher says "stand up," touch your nōse. →

the fat ēagle →

an ēagle līked to ēat. hē āte cāke and ham and →

cōrn. hē āte and āte, and hē got fatter and fatter. →

hē said, "I am sō fat that I can not flȳ." →

hē sat in a trēē and the other ēagles māde fun of →

him. they said, "look at that fat, fat ēagle. hō, hō."

but then a tīger cāme hunting fōr ēagles. a little

ēagle sat under a trēē. the tīger went after the

little ēagle. the other ēagles yelled and yelled, but the

little ēagle did not hēar them.

stop

read the Items

1. when the teacher says "touch your feet," stand

up.

2. if the teacher says "gō," touch your ears.

the fat eagle

a fat, fat eagle was sitting in a tree when a tiger

came hunting for eagles. the tiger went after a

little eagle that was sitting under the tree. the other

ēagles yelled, but the little ēagle did not hēar them.

the fat, fat ēagle looked down and said, "I must sāve the little ēagle." sō hē jumped from the trēē. hē cāme down līke a fat rock on the tīger. and the tīger ran far awāy.

now the other ēagles do not māke fun of the fat, fat ēagle. they give him cāke and ham and cōrn.

this is the end.

rēₐd the Ītems ⟶

1. if the tēₐcher says "touch your nōse," touch
   your fēēt.

2. when the tēₐcher says "givₑ mē your book," givₑ
   the tēₐcher your book.

a man līked to gō fast ➤

a man līked to gō fast. hē went fast in his

car. hē walked fast and hē ran fast. hē ēven talked

fast. his wīfe did not līke him to gō sō fast. but hē

went fast.

hē sat down to ēat an egg and a fish cāke and a

mēat pīe. but hē āte sō fast that the egg slipped and

fell on his fēēt.

hē bent down fast and his nōse went into the ⟶

fish cāke. hē went to wīpe his nōse fast and hē hit ⟶

the mēat pīe. the mēat pīe hit his wīfe. ⟶

stop ⟶

rēₐd the Ītems ➤

1. when the tēₐcher says "touch your heₐd," hōld up your hands.

2. if the tēₐcher picks up a book, sāy "now."

a man līkₑd to gō fast ➤

a man did thĩngs fast. hē went fast in his car. hē walkₑd fast. hē talkₑd fast. hē ēven ātₑ fast. and when hē ātₑ, hē got egg on his fēēt and fish cākₑ on his nōse.

the man said, "I will slōw down. I will not do

thiñgs fast."

sō the man did not gō fast in his car. hē did

not walk fast. hē did not talk fast. and hē did not

ēat sō fast that hē got fish cāke on his nōse.

this is the end.